# Hard Times, Good Times in Oregon

---

## Recollections of the 1930s

# Hard Times, Good Times in Oregon

## Recollections of the 1930s

*by*
*William R. Lindley*

**Sunflower University Press**®

1531 Yuma (Box 1009), Manhattan, Kansas 66502-4228  USA

Printed in the United States of America on acid-free paper.

ISBN 0-89745-186-4

Cover:
Photograph of Portland, Oregon, by Northwest photographer
Ray Atkeson, courtesy of American Landscapes, Portland.

Edited by Amie J. Goins
Layout by Lori L. Daniel

*In Appreciation*

*of my parents, family, neighbors,*
*and of course librarians,*
*for their good examples in the trying 1930s.*

# Contents

# *Preface*

I RECENTLY READ that some Idaho high school students were going to try living the way people did during the decade of the Great Depression, the 1930s. After reading John Steinbeck's novel, *The Grapes of Wrath*, they had decided to experience, for a night, the life of those mean times.

They had gathered old boards and had built a shack that looked like the ones that used to dot the "jungle" in Sullivan's Gulch, just east of the Steel Bridge in Portland. Fortunately for the students, Idaho has only one-third the rainfall of western

Oregon. The newspaper picture showed that the students had built during a dry spell; a downpour would have taught them how to snug up their rickety shack in a hurry.

The adventurers probably didn't have to make many changes to their clothing, because scruffy duds are acceptable now. But in the Depression years, neatness was important — for reasons of respect, amongst others. And if *you* didn't care, your mother did.

For food, the students had hot dogs — that was about right for the '30s — and chickens, which actually should have been saved for a typical Depression-era Thanksgiving dinner.

*The Grapes of Wrath* was a good choice for a model. Steinbeck had drawn an assignment from the *San Francisco News* to write a series of articles about farm labor camps, and he had the benefit of research by a Farm Security Administration labor camp manager. Thus, the novel was based on detailed observation. But the Depression happened everywhere across America, of course, and in many different settings, so although the Steinbeck account is a useful one, it is only a partial representation of the decade.

The Idaho students had an advantage outdoors, because they already knew about the practical work of ranching, logging, and mining, often firsthand. Still, I wondered what anybody could say to make the Depression years more real. It seemed that someone ought to write a close-to-home account before those times were forgotten.

These essays from my personal recollections are meant to describe ordinary people and their attitudes of self-reliance and self-respect, which I think were important in getting them through so many difficulties. Of course, it might be noted that there was no choice but to be self-reliant, though I'd say that no matter how the attitude originated, it was valuable.

But now it's time to put aside the present and step back to

the start of the 1930s. I'll point out some interesting things about my home neighborhood of Errol Heights and other places around Portland and Oregon, including the grand and the gritty. However, I'm well aware of the fact that although I grew up during the Depression, I didn't have to manage the hardest part — making ends meet.

William R. Lindley
Boise, Idaho

# The Empire
# Building Stops

*Land of the Empire Builders,*
*Land of the Golden West. . . .*

SCHOOL CHILDREN by uncounted thousands have sung those words to the state song, "Oregon, My Oregon," a rousing march adopted by the Legislature in 1927. The same heroic theme has been hailed in Oregon pageants and verse. It is the state's myth-like story of settlement and growth. But about two years after the Legislature endorsed the song, progress stumbled to a halt.

It wasn't just an Oregon happening, of course. The Depression swept the country, starting in the fall of 1929, even as financial experts were declaring the economy "fundamentally sound." Without warning, great numbers of people were jobless and thrown back on their own resources.

Government couldn't help much. At that time, there was no unemployment pay, no Social Security. Banks were in trouble, and certainly not about to lend money to people who had no income. Stores began to put up signs, which soon appeared everywhere: "Credit Makes Enemies. Let's Be Friends." Not even a dime was spent carelessly.

This book is about Oregon, especially Portland, during those years, the long decade of the 1930s. Much misinformation about those times has been printed. Some people think that during the Depression everyone went around *feeling* depressed. If that was so, they certainly didn't act that way. The idea was to hold your head high, not admitting you couldn't deal with the problems. Popular songs were more upbeat than they were later, when times improved. No wonder people are confused now about the Depression.

Much more so than today, people were on their own. Sociology and psychology hadn't attained the places they have now in education and popular "how to" books, explaining and excusing away problems. People were used to being more active, more self-sufficient. Adults of the 1930s had grown up in families of four to six children, where everyone had to lend a hand. They had grown up when transportation was by horse, not automobile, and it took much more effort to hitch up a horse than to turn an ignition key. It is ironic that today's affluent society is loaded with counseling and support groups, dealing with questions of self-esteem and the management of personal problems.

In the 1930s, people in Oregon still had some of the pioneer spirit, and they needed their independence, because when they turned to government, they found only confusion.

President Herbert Hoover, the orphan boy who had worked

hard and had become a millionaire, was supposed to apply the ideas of successful management to the country's ills, but the crisis was beyond him. His successor, Franklin D. Roosevelt, though experienced in politics as governor of New York, had no real plans. His New Deal approach was to try anything, and this may have had the benefit of assuring the hard-pressed citizens that somebody was helping.

Roosevelt described himself as a quarterback, writes historian Richard Hofstadter, but football is a game in which chance plays a large part. Hofstadter adds:

> The New Deal never will be understood by anyone who looks for a single thread of policy, a far-reaching, far-seeing plan. It was a series of improvisations, many adopted very suddenly, many contradictory. Such unity as it had was in political strategy, not economics.

So, while the natural reaction now is to ask why someone didn't do something about the crisis, the fact is that much *was* done at the time, but without early success. When even the supposed experts didn't know the answers, the public confidence surely must have been affected.

The Depression of the '30s arrived with a jolt. The country hadn't had such an experience for decades, and most of the financial crises in U.S. history had been relatively brief. But in 1929, there was no warning. Times seemed to be good, and our Errol Heights neighborhood no doubt was a fine place for its young families. After all, an *Oregonian* article had said that few East Side neighborhoods were more beautiful or promising, describing ours as a "natural park," and noting that the developer was even providing free streetcar service on a one-mile line from Eastmoreland to 52nd Avenue. It also described homes "erected along modest lines."

Experts now say that they find data showing that the country's financial structure was, in fact, shaky. Such information can help in providing answers to ongoing questions about what started the Depression. It could even contribute to plans for avoiding another disaster. However, a certain recklessness in high finance has continued. That is of concern to those who remember 1929, when in Oregon the empire building stopped.

# A Grand Setting

THE UNINSPIRED routines of daily life in Portland during the Depression were carried on in a natural setting of such grandeur that the citizens should have been dressed as for some great drama.

The Willamette River Valley, in which Portland lies, is a spread of greenery, breaking in gentle waves over the land and into nearby wooded hills. Just west of Portland is Council Crest, where Indians gathered in storied times, before the covered wagons. The river itself is named for an Indian tribe, the Wallamet.

East of Portland, the foothills form a stage for some real mountains, made all the more impressive because the valley is not many feet above sea level. The Rocky Mountains are often seen from an elevation of 5,000 feet or more. Near Portland, however, the mountains tower above the city's elevation of around 100 feet.

Mount Hood stands alone on Portland's eastern horizon, soaring to 11,239 feet in a sharp peak, with just enough roughness in its slopes to keep it from being mistaken for an oil painting. Sunrise and sunset tint its snows, sometimes in glowing rose, but a wintery morning may bring a dramatic frosted-pale lemon color to this massive sentinel.

In the 1930s, the popularity of skiing with its expensive waxed boards and chair lifts for the upward glide had not yet arrived, and Mount Hood mainly drew visitors for its climbing trails and scenery.

Another mountain, distinctive in a different way, stood across the Columbia River in Washington, clearly visible from Portland — Mount St. Helens, alone and majestic, with its beautiful snowy cone recalling the ancient times of erupting volcanoes.

It might even be said that these two mountains, with their massive forms unchanged over the years, gave a kind of assurance to those who admired their profiles from afar. There, in an uncertain world, Nature showed that some things would stay the same.

There was a reason why these mountains lent the effect of a smooth, majestic backdrop to daily events. We never got close enough to them to know their jumbled slopes and massive walls of stone, their ancient forests and brilliant streams. The reason we kept distant was expense. Anything beyond the reach of a city bus or bicycle was too far. The Pacific Ocean was only about 75 miles from Portland by highway, but many families had never seen its tumbling surf. My father could describe his years at sea, but the family's ideas of the ocean often were taken from pictures in encyclopedias.

But from the great snowfields on those mountains of the Cascade Range, the rivers reached us, dashing over rocky slopes and then rippling and gliding into meadowlands, and finally merging the traces of high winter storms into the currents of the Columbia, the "River of the West." It still rolled its mighty waters into the sea during those years, over rocky barriers in huge rapids, which blocked river traffic, at first forcing travelers to take portages and later the bypass of the Cascade Locks. Who would have guessed that a stairstep of dams would turn the Columbia into a series of huge mill ponds?

Along the south wall of the Columbia, on the Oregon side, sparkling waterfalls and mossy dells among the old firs provided the traveler with refreshing scenes, and, fortunately, that setting hasn't changed.

# *What the 1930s Hadn't*

A GOOD WAY to introduce the differences of life in the 1930s is to illustrate what was and wasn't available. Many conveniences of today didn't exist, and others were beyond scrimpy finances.

### What the 1930s had:

A lot of walking. No jogging.

Plenty of ironing. (There were no wash-and-wear clothes until 1940.)

A lot of shoe repair; not many new purchases.
All kinds of radio programs — news, comedy, quizzes, music.
Big gardens, with plenty of vegetables.
Home canning, especially of fruits.
Cooking in many homes on kitchen woodstoves, which also
    were a source of heat — sometimes the only source.
Jigsaw puzzles.
Chinese restaurants.
Canned milk.
More bad colds and other illnesses. (Antibiotics like penicillin
    weren't produced until the 1940s.)
Steam locomotives blasting out coal smoke. Factory smoke
    would have been welcome.


### And now on the other side:

No credit cards.
No power lawn mowers.
No jet planes. (Flying was for the wealthy, anyway.)
No diet centers. (Getting *enough* to eat was the problem.)
No exercise clubs — not when there was so much walking to
    do.
No television — not even black and white.
No skiing, except for the wealthy.
No pizza; no tacos.
No electric guitars.
No stereos.
No taped music (but 78 rpm records).
Not much made of plastic.
No telephone or refrigerator for many families.
Practically no vacations.
Few appointments with doctors and dentists; few eye and
    hearing examinations.

No contact lenses.
Few divorces.
No legal beer or other alcohol until 1933.


That final item needs some explanation. The U.S. Constitution was amended in 1919 to prohibit the making and distributing of alcoholic drinks, bringing the saloon era to an end. It was a step as drastic as if the country would today ban all tobacco.

The result was many kinds of illegal manufacture and bootleg distribution. In Portland, a greenhouse might deliver a bottle hidden in a plant. The illegal stuff could be dangerous, as the buyer didn't know how it had been made. A boozer in Yakima spilled some on his car and the next day the paint was gone from the spot.

Prohibition was repealed in 1933, which also happened to be the worst year of the Depression, and along 52nd Avenue in Errol Heights, the blue neon signs for Olympia beer glowed from the windows of taverns, by then referred to as "beer joints."

The fact is that while, in my recollection, people didn't talk much about politics, they sometimes remarked approvingly of FDR: "Well, he brought back beer."

I remember a favorite grade school joke about Prohibition in which a teacher is quizzing a young pupil:


Teacher: Who made the sun shine?
Child: God.
Teacher: Who made the stars shine?
Child: God.
Teacher: Who made the moon shine?
Child: Pa and the next-door neighbor!

That is not to say that the forces of temperance gave up; the frowning about alcohol continued in many circles.

Basically, new things were missing on the Depression scene. The brake had been put on all change. The farmer who was about to give up the horse-drawn plow in 1929 and buy a tractor likely was still working with a team in 1939. His wife's best coat was not replaced, but mended. The growing children had to have roomier clothes, of course. Hand-me-downs were the answer, and the youngest at times got some pretty tattered duds.

Around the neighborhood, there were no newcomers, no new houses or new cars, new employment, new streets, new hopes. It was the decade of the secondhand store. But as long as you could adapt to the ongoing sameness and be happy with a new candy bar or a new magazine, you could get by. That was true especially of kids, who had never known anything else.

# Food, Clothing, and Rain

ERHAPS RAIN should be mentioned first: how the wind gusts whipped it against the steamy windows for what seemed like week after week, as the kitchen woodstove flickered with an orange light from beneath the pans, keeping us warm and dry. Home was where you kept out of the rain, and dried your coats and your water-soaked shoes and socks.

There was rain of many kinds — misty rain or driving rain, the blustery rain that buffeted umbrellas, and now and then a shower with sunshine beaming through — the happiest kind of rain.

On some days, the rain might pour from the skies by the hour. You could tell who the natives were if you watched the crowded sidewalks downtown on a rainy day. When the first drops sprinkled in, the newcomers would dash to get under the awnings in front of the stores. But the locals showed no sign of knowing the weather had changed. After all, the rain might splash down for hours, so the reasonable thing to do was keep on about your business.

A prevailing southwest wind drove the rain in from the Pacific Ocean, 60 miles away. Sometimes the rain arrived in Portland in great folds of wetness, or again as a drizzle, like a morning on the beach. On other days it spattered the land and bounced in clusters of spray from the paved roads and side-walks. Errol Heights didn't have any pavement, so the rain just made more mud.

As the low, gray clouds swept eastward from the Willamette Valley, they soon reached the Cascade Range, and as they were forced up toward the snowfields at the peaks, they sloshed down nearly all of their moisture on the west side of the mountains as rain or snow. Within an hour's drive east of the summit was country so dry that the main shrub was sage-brush. Sometimes the rain was so mild that it was almost warm, but in winter it could feel more freezing than snow.

And then it was time for a hearty meal — no salads or snacks. And my mother's skill with the groceries meant there was always enough to eat. However, when it came to meat and potatoes, the emphasis was on potatoes. In our house there was meat for two meals a week, typically Saturday night and Sunday dinner, and the choices usually were hamburger and stew meat. At that, we counted ourselves better off than many families, though we were almost unintentional vegetarians, with our frequent meals of potatoes, carrots, onions, and tomatoes. Tomatoes (canned from our garden) with macaroni made a frequent dish. The main beverage was tea (coffee at breakfast), with milk now and then.

The fruit trees provided a bounty for pies and puddings, like brown betty — apples, bread crumbs, sugar, butter (if any), and spices.

My mother made bread in substantial loaves, and a few of those tasty slices could be a good part of a meal. Needless to say, "fancying up" the food to coax people to eat was unheard of (except for the ill), and nobody left anything on the plate. If the rain was rattling on the windows, steaming, homemade food tasted even better. A basic dish like oven-baked scalloped potatoes in a thick cheese sauce like cheddary custard made grand fare.

And while everyone was putting away the food, our clothes were drying for another trip out into the rain.

It didn't rain in summer, however. From late June through beaming mid-summer and into September, the skies were blue and the mud dried into dust that curled up in clouds as an occasional car bounced along the neighborhood's dirt roads.

Then one day in late September, someone would come into the house with the surprise report: "It's raining!"

# Holding on to a Job

*The boss may not always be right, but he's always the boss.*

THAT SAYING shows how, in the 1930s, the hope of keeping a job was constant. Differ with the boss, and you could be out in the street. A friend told me that his father spent an entire career in a detested job, just to feed the family. An employee didn't hope for advancement, only that the company somehow would stay in business.

Historian Terence O'Donnell notes that Oregon was not hit as hard as states where autos, steel, and textiles were major payrolls, but the situation was bad enough. Some entire towns had been built around a single lumber mill, but few houses were going up anywhere. Many businesses were owned by a local family, with a few others on the payroll who were almost like family; then a decision to lay someone off wasn't made by distant management, but painfully close to home.

A woman I know tells of how she would hear her folks, who owned a neighborhood grocery in Montana, talk over some wrenching decisions. Should a hard-up neighbor get more credit? If not, the family might go hungry. But if the store owners helped too many people, there'd be no cash for the next truckload of groceries. The wholesaler might need the money to pay on a loan, and the bank couldn't wait because it had to pay clerks and buy fuel to fend off the icy Montana winters. Presumably the grocery store's prices already had been marked way down to hold on to customers who counted every coin.

Gradually, the government began to provide jobs. The Civilian Conservation Corps (CCC) sent young men to forest camps. They built bridges, trails, shelters, and campgrounds, which still add to the pleasure of parks and scenic places. Nationally, the Works Progress Administration (WPA), later Work Projects Administration, constructed more than 650,000 miles of roads, plus buildings and other structures. Included were federal programs for artists, writers, and people in the theater, plus a National Youth Administration for teenagers.

All of this federal assistance, important as it was, ran counter to the traditional self-reliance which people had developed. Some were unhappy to accept help, but as the months and years of scrimping went on, they had no choice, and it wasn't until 1935 that the WPA was established, after several years of the Depression.

It must also be noted that today's safety nets for the jobless and the elderly did not exist when the Depression began. The Social Security Act was passed in 1935 and payroll withholding for it started in 1937, but the first checks were not mailed until January 1940, near the end of the Depression. Unemployment compensation was part of the Social Security Act, administered by the states. The first check was written in 1937. However, only people who had worked for a contributing employer were covered. So, with no safety nets available to those who had lost their jobs or wanted to retire, everyone who was employed worked hard to stay that way. This meant that there was no turnover to provide openings for young people who were ready to work.

Years later, while on a news staff in Portland, I heard about a young woman who had landed a job, despite those limitations.

She had earned a journalism degree at the University of Oregon, so, logically enough, she walked into an editor's office one day and said she was applying for a job. It happened that she had a name that was well known locally; she wouldn't have gone hungry without employment, but she wanted a job.

The editor pointed out the realities of the Depression: no one was likely to leave newsroom employment in the predictable future. But the young lady persisted, promising to start right away. She even offered to work for nothing, sweep out the place — anything connected with journalism.

In journalism, initiative and persistence are valued; after all, those traits get the news. Finally, the editor told her that she could practice some news work, and soon she was making herself useful. Eventually, the inevitable happened — someone got sick, and there she was, trained and ready to go.

Maybe that's not much of a story today, in years when

people are particular about employment, but our staff admired
this young woman because of what she had accomplished,
despite the impossible times.

# *Ideal Life in Eastmoreland*

WE TRUDGED to school along the muddy roads from Errol Heights, crossing onto the edge of Eastmoreland, that well-trimmed neighborhood of ideal American homes. We were something like trespassers. In Eastmoreland, every street was paved from curb to curb with thick asphalt, and holes in the pavement were unknown to children who played street hockey on clattering skates. Artfully curved sidewalks swept past two-story homes clad in white paint or sturdy brick.

Neatness was everywhere. When leaves fell in autumn,

crews with huge brooms swept them from the gutters, and as trucks cruised by, the men scooped up the soaked leaves and swung them on board, restoring the tidy atmosphere.

Every lawn in Eastmoreland was trimmed like part of an extensive park, unlike the neighborhood of scruffy lots where we lived, back along the muddy roads.

In Eastmoreland, no curl of old paint was permitted to show itself for long; soon the house was brushed with fresh color. Each one looked new, like those in model villages that architects set up, with the toy shrubs in front. It was a stage setting for life as it should be, and it didn't take much to imagine the spacious rooms, like pictures in *Better Homes and Gardens*, where the silver coffee service gleamed on the sideboard and children happily stroked the wiry coats of black Scotty dogs.

Alongside one street of homes was a handsome golf course, and for some reason it was public, not private. There were no parks to mention, but the generous lawns and tree-shaded streets provided cool settings. A motorway called Reed College Place had a large divider of lawn to separate the traffic lanes. At the end of this boulevard, Reed College and its formal brick buildings stood at the forested edge of several ponds, where swans coolly glided.

Portland evidently had gone through a stage of naming residential districts after places in novels like those of Sir Walter Scott, embracing Eastmoreland, Westmoreland, Laurelhurst, Irvington, Ardenwald, Dunthorpe, and Garthwick — each conveying a grandness that had been appropriate in the 1920s. In those times, who wouldn't want to stretch the family finances a bit to reside in such a district, when prosperity was so evident? There would still be enough left each month to pay the maid and for other necessities in places like Eastmoreland.

The same optimism must have run like springtime through rural tracts such as Errol Heights, separated by a truck garden from Eastmoreland. True, the streets weren't paved and a house might be covered with tarpaper on the outside — but that, of course, was temporary, because there were steady jobs to be had. So the war veterans and their young wives and families worked in the yards and gardens and no doubt anticipated street lighting, paving, neighborhood parks, and other good things not far ahead.

Actually, what was not far ahead was the Depression. But it was odd how nothing in Eastmoreland seemed to change, at least on the outside. Were these people exempt from the unemployment? Life in Eastmoreland seemed as enviable as before.

I kept that impression for years, though I didn't see much of Eastmoreland after I went to high school. But then I happened to hear from a woman who had lived during the '30s in what she called one of the "richer areas," but where there were "people like us who were so dreadfully poor that we have stinging memories, too. The Depression days which we went through and the panic of hearing the grown-ups at home continually wondering where enough money would come from — has colored my life ever since," she wrote, some 35 years after the Depression ended.

Much effort went into the carefully staged lifestyles of those times. We're told of a mother gathering her children behind a curtain and keeping them quiet while the milkman rang to collect the bill. And at one such home with an overdue bill, a child knew the milkman's daughter, a gossipy classmate at school.

There were probably similar happenings in Eastmoreland.

# *Down by the Tracks*

THE FASCINATION of the mighty steam locomotive — a dinosaur of the machine age — is incomparable now, because nothing is nearly so primitive as the effect of a long, low whistle in the distance, the gathering thunder of the great wheels, the black smoky plume flung into the air, and that huge mass of steel hurtling right at you, held on its course only by two narrow ribbons of track. In an instant it is right there and gone, leaving you with an image of the most astonishing contrast, of ladies and gentlemen dining without care in a luxurious restaurant that glides by, while in other cars there are travelers of all kinds, with varied expressions, casually watching the scenery roll past.

The railroads then — steam, in the 1930s, not chugging diesels — had a special appeal. You could walk right up to them in town or country. Of course, sometimes we would see an airplane, humming along between horizons like a big dragonfly. But to see an airplane up close would have required traveling to the airport. This kind of trip seldom was made by families without a car. On the other hand, the Southern Pacific tracks were just down Johnson Creek, and along them a mile or so were the Brooklyn yards, where the peppy switch engines shunted cars around, making up the long trains to which the powerful road locomotives finally would be coupled. At night, the flickering orange fireboxes of the engines rolling along under the yard lights gave a certain kind of ancient drama to the scene.

Because this was before the neat, honking diesels, coal smoke drifted in the air, with its bracing tang. Whistle blasts cleared the way as engines rumbled past, dragging strings of rattling cars. Lanterns with handles like pails were swung along the cars at night, as trainmen made inspections. The action rolled around the clock. Call boys (in some places, anyway) made sure crews didn't oversleep, pounding on doors in the middle of the night. The boy couldn't accept a mumbled "All right," or some less polite answer. The rule was not to leave until the trainman was on his feet.

The kids from Errol Heights had a favorite stop at the yards in summer — a sidetrack where watermelons were unloaded. We were always hoping that one had been dropped accidently, and could be discarded in our direction. We did well in that SP melon patch.

Watching the changing yard activity was great, because you never knew where the trains were going. In the 1930s, automobiles were not used for most long trips. It was the railroad that sent its colorful cars rumbling across rivers and through steep mountains to the gleaming cities, and to smooth beaches where palm trees fringed an exotic scene, like the kind in a slick copy of *The Saturday Evening Post.*

Railroaders gave the whole enterprise a human touch. An engineer always waved to kids along the tracks. The engineer was not a cardboard hero, but the friendly rider of a charging black locomotive. We never thought of him as a man thinking about home, where the lawn needed mowing, because he always was there in the cab of the mighty steam engine — you usually didn't get close to a rolling locomotive, and from a distance all the engineers looked the same.

It seemed like a great life, and many a kid wanted to become an engineer. Of course, we didn't know that the sensible diesels were going to replace the steamers and crimp the style of veteran railroaders. We also didn't know the dangers that lay beyond the yards, of working on icy cars in winter, and of summers so hot that they buckled steel rails; it was even hotter up there behind the firebox. It seemed to us that this was a life of clambering up the ladders and rolling along the line to happy places like the painted towns in storybooks.

# No Dimes to Spare

❦

"BROTHER CAN You Spare a Dime?" is a song that is often played on programs depicting the Depression days. It's more dramatic than most popular music, but I don't recall hearing it during the 1930s. People probably didn't want the reality of their lives sung to them. However, I do remember numerous songs about hope, dreams that might come true, wishing on a star, greeting the dawn, the new day, the sun, and so on — all optimistic.

On the radio, comedy shows were the favorites, with the entertainers taking people's minds off those scarcely hopeful days. "Amos 'n' Andy" was so popular that movie theaters had to interrupt their films to broadcast the show; otherwise, people would go home to listen. Comedians who successfully brought their vaudeville stage acts to radio included Jack Benny, Eddie Cantor, and Fred Allen. The shows were all clean, lively, family entertainment.

Occasionally on the streets a tramp would ask if you could spare a dime, but there didn't seem to be much of that. Perhaps it was a waste of time when people were watching even their nickels closely. I remember tramps coming up to Aunt Laura's place in Eugene, not far from the Southern Pacific main line, and asking for something to eat. They were always polite and often suggested they'd be willing to help with some chore. She'd size them up, sometimes have them chop wood for the cookstove, sometimes just give them food. Many were, after all, family men looking for jobs. Presumably, those were the times that had originated the farewell, "Write if you get work." At the depth of the Depression in 1933, about one-third of the work force was unemployed.

Many knew that there was work to do around a rural place, because in those days a lot of it had to be done by hand, and even energetic people needed help. Gardens were hoed, not tilled with a motorized rig; lawns and plants were weeded, not sprayed with chemicals; tall grass had to be cut with a sickle; and wood needed to be chopped. People who worked hard preferred to hand out dimes when they had been earned.

Working in Depression-era shops and mills also required strength and endurance — lifting heavy loads, turning hand wrenches, sledgehammering iron, stacking green lumber. There were no fork lifts, power wrenches, pneumatic hammers, or chain saws available. Men sometimes had permanent limps, bruised hands, scars, or lingering coughs. Work places might be smoky, dusty, or dangerous, but with jobs so scarce, it would have been risky to mention it.

Women worked equally hard, and often quoted the lines:

> A man works from sun to sun,
> but a woman's work is never done.

Anyone who questioned that (and I can't recall anyone so reckless) would have been told a long list of household duties, many of which don't even exist today.

As an example, ironing, among the least-favorite tasks, could take a whole day before wash-and-wear and permanent-press fabrics were developed.

Home canning would last all summer, off and on, as new crops became ripe. For most people, the idea of buying a jar of jam at the store would have been foolish. Most families had a few fruit trees, or for 75 cents or $1 could buy a bushel of apples or peaches (a bushel was much larger than today's typical store box). In it was local, ripe fruit too, not stuff picked half green so it could be freighted across the country.

Most clothing was sewn at home, and there was the never-ending darning of socks and patching of anything wearable. To such women, today's household with automatic washing, drying, power cleaning, and instant cooking would seem a marvel. Only caring for children seems to require about the same amount of time as ever, but in today's households there are fewer of them.

As for the men, they probably would think today's supposedly tiring efforts in committee meetings and with electronic gizmos scarcely qualify as work, and the idea of going to a health club in order to get some exercise might seem unbelievable.

# Blue Collars
# and Crafts

BLUE COLLARS were everywhere in Depression years on pick-and-shovel jobs. There were ditches to dig, brush to pull up, wheelbarrows to push, fields to hoe. There was lumber to load, coal to shovel, wood to saw by hand, grass to rake. Not much machinery was used on these jobs. To buy it and run it cost money. People would work cheap, and were glad to have some coin.

Men riding home on the 52nd Avenue bus in Portland sometimes looked more than tired, almost dazed, maybe with red-rimmed eyes from smoke or cinders. Beside them sat women who had clerked all day in stores — spending many hours on their feet, being polite and helpful to people who had a few dimes to spend. Women at home had it no easier; some still made do with washboards for the laundry and pressed clothes with heavy sadirons, which were heated on woodstoves.

Not all were involved in everyday labor, of course. There were people who did skilled craft work — cabinetmakers, wood carvers, metal workers, and sign painters. These skills typically were learned by apprenticeship, not from books. In fact, there was some suspicion of using books as a way of acquiring a craft — but this was not a prejudice against reading, writing and arithmetic. My Uncle Art, who had drilled water wells around Eugene for years, brushed aside the theories of geology professors. He knew the land; he could find water. He also sharpened drill bits weighing (as I recall) up to 400 pounds at his glowing forge.

This was the legacy of the apprenticeship system — of learning by years of doing the work, guided by those who had mastered it. This was individual instruction, with each task given the personal touch. Practical problems were solved by using past experience and reasoning, not by looking up the answers. Work was not standardized. Personal independence was valued.

The hours were long, but, in the best of such shops, the teamwork used in getting the job done made the effort worthwhile.

But Henry Ford's assembly line pointed to change. In his plants, no talking or any behavior that interfered with the monotonous work on the moving line was permitted, and spotters around the plants made sure that no casual remark or laugh was heard. Certainly Ford's Model T was a breakthrough in transportation and lifestyle, but its standardized look and low cost had a price — the way the work was done.

In fact, Ford preferred not to hire skilled craftsmen at all.

Perhaps some may think that work in the Depression days required less ability than subsequently, but people who had to solve all kinds of practical problems from experience actually employed much intelligence. If they needed assistance, they turned to others they respected. In the Depression, anything that broke had to be repaired. The practice of simply replacing whole parts had not been developed, and when labor was cheap, fixing was the least expensive option.

What about the white-collar workers? They were a much smaller group in the years when less than 40 percent of high-school students completed their studies, and not many of those went on to college. The destiny of most youth in the Depression was a blue-collar job.

But understanding the Depression means knowing about the work and how it set the tone of daily life, with long hours of labor, even in the crafts. In retailing, few stores were fran-chised; each place had the personality of its owner and the "hired help." These people were individuals with their own capable or quirky ways, not products of some standardized national training program. Customers also were individuals. A grocer might say on the phone, "Mrs. Rogers, those peaches you wanted have just come in. We could deliver a crate this afternoon."

Work then had its minuses, too. Looking back on my par-ents' generation, it seemed people really were middle-aged by their 40s. The heavy chores of farm and factory, of home and family, had worn them, leaving limps, scars, perhaps recurring pains, and a certain weariness. Further, the groceries that people could afford often ran to the cheap, starchy foods; people took on a stocky appearance around middle age, referred to as "heavyset."

Those were the days in which not cranking an automobile

properly would cause the crank to swing back and break an arm. I never knew of this happening, but the overall impression was that, in many ways, life then was considerably harder, and the days longer.

Take the basics of everyday life: food, clothing, and shelter. Meals often were prepared from scratch. The first quick-meal items, frozen food and cake mixes, were not introduced until around 1949; from these, fast food was developed. Sewing often was done at home, and mending was frequent when there was no money for new clothcs. The quilts so much admired today also had the practical benefit of using up scraps of cloth from other projects. I can remember daughters looking over a quilt and recalling favorite dresses from the squares. Shelter? There was no new construction. Fixing things to last a while longer was the rule in those hard times.

# The Land of Opportunity

❧❧❧

THOSE DEPRESSION years must have brought a special unhappiness to families from overseas, to people who had risked everything on America's promise. They were part of the great wave of European immigration which peaked in 1900-1910 and was ended by hard times. The 1920 U.S. census listed a foreign-born population of nearly 20 percent in Portland. I knew the talk and customs of these people as a boy, though the old-country lifestyles often disappeared in a single generation. Many of these families had sold everything in their native country to seek new opportunities in America.

Newcomers to Oregon learned about the success of immigrants like Simon Benson, the lumber king who had landed in the United States from Norway before his 16th birthday almost penniless, and had built an empire on the lower Columbia River. They knew that in 1915 he gave the Portland School District $100,000 to start Benson Polytechnic School, and that he financed a hotel downtown as part of a personal campaign to promote the city and tourism.

Benson had learned rudimentary English in a few months after his arrival, and had received a bonus from his employer for doing so. That was the way new Americans cast aside the heritage of Europe, where people were tied to a class system that often held back their hopes for a better life.

Still, people who spoke German, Norwegian, Polish, or Danish sometimes settled together in Oregon neighborhoods, at times near a church where Scripture and hymns were brought from the old country.

It seems this pattern didn't persist for long, especially when there were marriages between nationalities. If the bride and groom were from a Danish background, for example, some Danish probably would be spoken in the new home, but if they represented separate cultures, they would communicate in the English they had learned in school. Their children, who might be embarrassed by old-country ways or simply not relate to them, would grow up fully Americanized.

There were other influences, too. On the U.S. comedy stage there was much parody of foreign traits. There was the Englishman with, "I say, old chap," the stingy Scot, the "*Ach, du lieber*" German, and the hand-kissing Frenchman, all with manners and accents grossly exaggerated. Crude as such humor was, it no doubt made immigrants discard traits that might attract attention. Of course, the American Southerner and Westerner, and other regional types were parodied, too. I can say honestly, however, that I never did hear any public disparagement of newcomers, but old country manners were disappearing fast as the Depression arrived.

The change is evident in what happened to the community of Danebo, west of Eugene. In 1900, a United Danish Lutheran Church pastor took an option on 1,280 acres there and invited settlers from the Midwest to buy portions of the tract. My Danish mother's family moved to that vicinity from Iowa about that time, but took land closer to Eugene. A church was built at Danebo and services were held in Danish. Gradually, English services were added, and by the 1930s there was only an infrequent service in Danish "for the old folks." Eugene annexed Danebo in the 1960s.

# *On the Sunny Side*

M UCH OF what I remember from the stories, poems, songs, and plays of Depression school days is sentimental. There was the impression that life was pleasant and promising, despite evidence everywhere to the contrary. No doubt some of this was a carryover by adults from their own happier years. My mother, who was a realist if there ever was one, would sing from her school days in Eugene:

> Good morning, merry sunshine,
> how did you wake so soon?

or a verse from another song that ended:

> But we'll be happy while in school
> though 'tis a rainy day.

Longfellow was the typical poet of our school days, and we read his tribute to the village blacksmith, though probably few of us had ever seen one. But it is the staunch character of the blacksmith on which the poem turns, and that seems to derive from hard work.

We sang the patriotic songs about our country, sometimes called Columbia, whose mandates made tyranny tremble, but to which the world offered homage.

So despite the country being in desperate circumstances, somehow our lives were pictured as fine. It doesn't make sense now, but it would have made less to feel sorry for ourselves. That is a luxury for those who are well off.

In high school, we read a lot of English literature by poets like Wordsworth and others, who had two themes, which now seem to have faded — the inspiration of Nature and the rare deeds of the individual.

Wordsworth could write of the scene from Westminster Bridge:

> Ships, towers, domes, theaters and temples lie
> Open unto the fields, and to the sky;
> All bright and glittering in the smokeless air.

Tennyson could take up the heroic theme of aging Ulysses:

> I cannot rest from travel; I will drink
> life to the lees. . . .
> Come, my friends,
> 'Tis not too late to seek a newer world.

It is surprising to realize now that we were being taught much that was a carryover from the Victorian era. My father grew up in England during the reign of Queen Victoria, which lasted until 1901. He still admired the deeds of the individual, and adventured on the high seas and in war. The message of the Depression, however, was that the individual could do almost nothing — that there were massive industrial and financial forces that were plunging the country into disaster; not even those at the helm understood what course to set. All one person could manage in such circumstances was to endure with as positive an attitude as possible.

I don't mean to imply that my father was a parlor Victorian; years of the rough sailor's life on towering square riggers obviously showed in how he reacted to hard times. Discipline in the face of trouble was his rule. Other neighbors presumably had learned the same lesson in one way or another, in times when there were no government handouts or legions of counselors.

Much of what we were taught was from books, and I doubt the schools had money for new editions in most cases; this, and the usual delays in getting material into print, would unavoidably mean some outdated instruction. But a major difference between then and now is television, which means seeing people and places as they are, right up to the minute. For children, this has meant that considerable knowledge, especially as to behavior, has not been filtered through adult standards. Parents no longer provide a child's introduction to the world — a gradual and selective process. Television has become an ongoing experience, a habit, and the content is simplified to maximize the number of viewers. There is no way for TV to deal with the individual, alone and thinking, absorbing the impressions of Nature. That content is for books, and in the Depression there was plenty of time for reading. Now the glib people of TV Land, with their constant talk, are a parody of thinking individuals, and an "anything goes" attitude takes the place of self-discipline. It indeed is remarkable that the negative experiences of the Depression brought about certain positive attitudes that are less noticeable today.

# *Making the Fun Last*

N O MATTER how skimpy the family income, kids somehow could scrounge the coins for tops, marbles, kites, fishing gear, a secret detective badge, roller-skating at Oaks Park, and sometimes roller coaster riding at Jantzen Beach.

When the money was gone, there was beachcombing on the Willamette and watching motorboats churn the river from the Sellwood Bridge; there was cheering at Journal Juniors amateur shows, swimming at city pools, playing Tarzan on the brushy lots, and munching wild hazelnuts and blackberries.

The sturdy Douglas firs that grew tall around the neighborhood in Errol Heights provided a good pastime for energetic kids. The limbs were strong, but not brittle like those of some trees, and ideally spaced for climbing. There was nothing to catch or scratch you as you clambered to the bendy top, where you could sway in the wind and holler to the neighborhood.

In the nearby woody brush grew hazelnut, dogwood, wild cherry, and other trees — some good for fishing poles, some for bows, and some for arrows or spears.

Among the hobbies was collecting lead foil from cigarette packages. We were regular scavengers when it came to that, but what anybody did with the big lead-foil balls I don't know.

There was an odd fad involving cellophane, a thin and transparent plastic. This was folded into strips and woven into belts of various color combinations, which, as I recall, were seldom worn.

Among novelties, there were books only about four inches square but perhaps two inches thick, with facing pages having a comic strip-type drawing and a few words. The stories were about our favorites from the comics or movies.

We were great coupon clippers, sending away for such items as a miniature can of Postum or a few spoonfuls of cereal — absolutely free. And there were kids' clubs sponsored by cereal companies, sometimes named for a comic strip detective. You got a tin badge, a book about secret codes (to foil bad guys), a certificate to show you officially did secret work, and probably a pitch for buying more cereal.

Some of the comic strip characters also were featured in radio programs broadcast right after school.

Music as a pastime could begin with a rattling guitar made from a cigar box. However, in the closets of many homes there often was a forgotten bugle, mandolin, ukulele, or something, and a kid would figure out how to make noise with it. We cranked up quite a racket. On summer evenings, we played outdoors for the benefit of the entire neighborhood — our parents may have suggested the location.

Bicycles were for sport and transport, and that was before there were various gear ratios, so we alternately cruised and puffed our way through miles of green countryside. Biking was safer then, with fewer cars on the roads. Probably half the families in our neighborhood had no car, and those with one watched the cost of gasoline.

Even the rain provided something to do, making huge puddles in the streets, which hadn't known gravel for years, if ever. It was fun to scratch channels in the mud between puddles, through which the water rushed in marvels of kid engineering.

Downhill our muddy rivers ran to Johnson Creek. There, on an adventure hike, we might find a battered raft in the willows and push out into the ripples, though we never got far because of the gravel bars and muddy shallows. Not many fish made the upstream trip, either, but we could lift rocks and watch the crawfish scurry away. Now and then the quiet would be blasted by the horn of an interurban streetcar headed between Gresham and downtown, another world far from our brushy trails.

One of the differences in youthful play then was that it was so active. It was a mile to a city swimming pool, so the swim and walk (or bike ride) both were healthy. The idea of a parent taking a kid somewhere (if the family had a car) would have been thought absurd. There also were ball games. When rain frequently drove kids indoors, making music was a favorite choice, along with playing board games, like checkers. Occasionally a well-worn record or two might be played. Radio was reserved for one or two programs during the day; no background music was played constantly. Kids alone often turned to reading, which, of course, helped to improve their school work. The shortage of money shaped this pattern. Every record got played hundreds of times, and nearly every book eventually was read.

The picture of today's kids hassling their parents for the latest toy, declaring in stores that they won't settle for anything but the newest cereal, showing up for skiing in the latest color, and expecting to be chauffeured everywhere is a complete contrast with the almost Victorian rules for children of the 1930s, which emphasized sensible behavior and some enjoyable independence.

# Of 52nd Avenue and Independence Day

MOST PEOPLE in Portland never had heard of Errol Heights, but that wasn't surprising. It had no bright lights, unless you counted the neon signs in taverns on 52nd Avenue, and skyrockets on the Fourth of July. A kid could slurp a pineapple milkshake mixed by the pharmacist at 52nd and Flavel, and hear about his boy ripping up the yards on the Oregon State football team, the closest to fame that anybody in the neighborhood got, as far as I heard.

As for cultural events, you might hear some boys blasting the reeds on their harmonicas. "Wreck of the Old 97" was a favorite, complete with chuffing imitations in the low notes and whistles in the high ones. Sometimes the boys would edge into the taverns, pluck guitar and banjo and catch a few coins — parents frowned when they found out, but not much. Coins were too scarce.

There were also secondhand stores. Some of the items for sale might be called antiques now, but Depression shoppers wanted useful, cheap merchandise; antiques were things at your grandma's house. People could spend a lot of time at secondhand stores trying to get a dime or two knocked off the price of some worn hunk of hardware.

The surprising thing was how money could be whisked out of hiding for special times. Coins and a bill or two — which, by every account, did not exist the day before — were discovered by the Fourth of July, a day which popped with excitement every year, when no laws stopped kids from blasting away with huge crackers, or whirling sparkling chunks of light into the sky.

The fireworks stands on 52nd Avenue did a brisk business, mainly with kids, who touched off a few firecrackers right away, and then fanned into the neighborhood for a rattling afternoon.

The truly memorable Independence Day celebration in our neighborhood was held by the German-Americans, who showed a gusto that was perfect for the occasion.

About sundown, they would set out a row of chairs on a family's lawn. In front would be a washtub full of ice, crowded with bottles of beer. Amid friendly talk, the bottles were tilted often, and anticipation grew as twilight dimmed the sky. As soon as it was dark, a great bundle of skyrockets was brought out. Then came the launching of the first rocket, as a sputtering match was touched to the fuse. Suddenly a brilliant gold train of fire streaked skyward as the rocket soared, and the crowd let out a long "Ahhhhh!" Then came more beer, another rocket, and another "Ahhhhh." It continued into the night, uncomplicated and satisfying. The occasion required no speeches, no ceremony, nothing special but the rockets' red glare on the glorious Fourth.

# Before Life
# Got Complicated

ONE OF the unusual sights I remember from Depression days was that of a man taking apart an automobile engine. I had seen men work on cars before, but the methodical way this home mechanic went at his project was different. He spread a large piece of canvas on the lawn beside his house, took the engine apart, washed each piece (probably in kerosene), and laid it on the canvas. Eventually, he had all the pieces in neat rows. Then he greased each one and put the engine back together.

Things weren't so complicated in those days. The radio was

the most advanced equipment in most households, and it was provided with vacuum tubes, which were sold in stores, meaning that the owner could fix at least one common problem.

A few tradesmen made their way through the neighborhood now and then to do work with special equipment.

There was the man who had a gasoline-powered saw on the back of his truck to cut longer pieces of firewood into lengths that would fit a woodstove. The zinging of the saw carried through the neighborhood. After the wood was sawed, the pieces were thrown into the basement (if the house had one), where they would be out of the rain.

The scissors grinder also showed up occasionally. I even saw an iceman carrying with tongs a block of clear ice, for use in iceboxes, before electric refrigerators arrived.

Some household items were peddled from door to door, among which were numerous extracts to flavor foods. But milk was not delivered to most of our neighbors, since many people used the condensed kind, which came to be known as the "iron cow."

The uncomplicated ways of those times probably worked out all right for the grown-ups, many of whom had been born between 1860 and 1900. They could recall a childhood where there was a hand pump on the back porch for drawing well water, a hammock providing summer air conditioning, slamming screen doors to keep out flies, and a front-porch rocker for evening relaxing. For entertainment, they had stereoscopes provided with three-dimensional photos, and magic lanterns which showed colored glass slides. Emphasis then was on lots of work, interspersed with simple pleasures.

The old definitions of work ran deep. I still recall a scene in the 1940s when I stopped to have coffee with my Aunt Laura, who lived on River Road, north of Eugene. My grandmother, who lived nearby, happened to walk in during our chat. She was around 90 and wore the full-skirted dresses of earlier times, which almost touched the floor; the colors were subdued with patterns in small designs.

Grandmother believed in work, and her daughters had been known to run into the garden to stop her from weeding in the hot sun when she was in her late 80s or early 90s.

Grandmother was from Denmark, and she and Aunt Laura chatted in Danish, which was just as well for me. Aunt Laura told me later that Grandmother had asked what kind of work I did — after all, here I was, sitting around at midafternoon. Aunt Laura replied that I went to university classes in the morning and was night editor on the *Register-Guard*. Evidently, Grandmother didn't think that scribbling at the newspaper was real work. She suggested I ought to be out painting the barn.

# The Dime Store Wonderland

I T IS difficult to imagine now the special place that stores like Woolworth's had in the Depression. During the days when "we can't afford it" was the answer to so many wishes, at the Five and Dime it was different. People who bought so much stuff at rummage sales and secondhand stores could wander the aisles where everything was brand new and affordable, even if the shopper had only a couple of quarters to spare.

This kind of selling wasn't started in the Depression. F. W. Woolworth had begun his stores decades earlier, at first with nothing priced over a nickel. This was raised to a dime, and when the Depression started, nothing on those red-front counters cost more than a dime. The limit was increased to 20 cents in 1932 and removed in 1935, after which prices were inched up, a nickel at a time, as management cautiously tested what its scrimping customers could pay.

In Portland, as in other cities, Woolworth's was right downtown on one of the best streets — a big, clean store, just as well run as the best department stores. Brightly lighted and bustling, it was a place where customers felt welcome, even in spending a dime.

It's impossible to sum up all the things those stores held.

As a kid, I would head straight for the candy counters, where you could get a sack of sweets for a dime. Nothing fancy, but all the basic and popular flavors of licorice, peppermint, red-hot cinnamon, and sour lemon drops. There were those chocolate discs with white sprinkles on top, orange-colored marshmallow bananas with real artificial flavor, marshmallow squares rolled in toasted coconut, crunchy chunks of peanuts mixed in hardened syrup, and, of course, gummy fudge. The cookies were nearby — sticky fig bars, spicy dutch windmills with almond slices on top, frosting-filled sandwiches, and marshmallow cookies dipped in chocolate. There were long counters full of the sweet stuff. It took patience for clerks to outwait kids choosing from so many treats.

Near the front of the store were displays of nail polish, makeup, perfume, and hair curlers, plus a hundred other items which guaranteed beauty. A Depression-era schoolgirl could "doll herself up," as they said then, on a budget. Her parents, of course, found more practical items at Woolworth's.

Deciding how to spend some change then was as serious as counting out paper money in more prosperous times.

# Back to the Farm

WHEN THE Depression gets attention these days, it is almost exclusively treated as a financial problem. The finances eventually righted themselves (there's not much indication that smart people deliberately managed the economy out of its nose dive), but some Depression-era changes became locked into the way people have lived since. The most important one, it seems to me, involves a reliance on the government for help with jobs, health, housing, and retirement, to name just a few basic items.

Today people are so used to this that it seems logical, but the

WPA was scorned and scoffed at to some extent when it was introduced in 1935. Many men felt that they were admitting defeat by signing up, but their hungry families gave them little choice. After all, there was no jobless pay, which has since become a basic support for those out of work. Medical, dental, health, and retirement expenses — all were among the individual's own personal responsibilities then.

Oddly enough, the "make work" projects of the WPA and CCC, which involved jobs that were not essential, and were shrugged off as excuses to put people on the government payroll, have benefited Oregon considerably. On many a country path, the walker may find a bridge or wall from those days, and some city buildings and post office murals have WPA origins.

I recall a photograph of a crew working along Johnson Creek in those days, mostly with shovels — no machinery in sight. A bulldozer could have speeded up the job, but of course that wasn't the idea. Nobody knew how long the Depression would last.

Well, how did people get by before there was all this government assistance? The answer had been around since ancient times. They depended on the family. In many households lived a son or daughter who hadn't married and had no income (and some stayed around when they had jobs, too). An elderly aunt might be a permanent resident; who could afford nursing homes? If, as the saying goes, "many hands make light work," there was plenty of help for the household chores, and babysitters were right there.

Families helped in other ways, too. My Aunt Laura sometimes mailed from Eugene a bowl-sized chunk of butter — she had a cow and a hand churn. Sometimes dried fruits and nuts were mailed from the farm — we didn't have a refrigerator.

Neighbors shared vegetables, fruits, and flowers from their

gardens, but regular family support was the key. Often sons and daughters who had married would live in the same community, frequently dropping by for a chat with relatives as part of daily life. In hard times, having someone to talk with can help a lot.

The family farm was a good place to be during the Depression. There you knew where the next meal was coming from — that is, from the land you had planted. In the city, the sidewalks couldn't give you any assurance.

The family farm was close to a self-supporting system, when large families did all the work of growing a variety of crops. This setup was so attractive that the national drift to the cities stopped during the Depression.

Oregon was settled by farmers, and, at first, they far outnumbered town people. In 1860, there were 50,000 people on farms and 3,000 in towns. Gradually, the number of town people increased, but it was not until 1930 that they took the lead over country people, with 490,000 Oregonians in cities and 464,000 in the country. Then, when the Depression continued, the country residents regained the lead, 558,000 to 532,000, holding it until after the hard times were over, when a strong trend to the cities developed. But programs introduced by the government during the Depression held on, and by then city people had something like a support system, with jobless pay and other benefits. Government had taken a new and extended role in the lives of everyone.

# *A Railroad Town's Story*

L IVING IN a town with a single kind of payroll has always meant some uncertainty. The busted gold-mining towns of eastern Oregon tell that story. There are farming centers where the price of a single crop or a change in rainfall decides everyone's future. The fishing villages know all about the verdict of the year's catch. And then there are railroad towns like Huntington, where the big trains roll in around the clock.

With their work of moving freight and passenger traffic across the nation, railroad towns reflect the relative prosperity of the rest of the country.

Huntington's location was decided by railroads. Flat land was required for a switchyard where two lines joined, at the Snake River Bridge between Oregon and Idaho. That free-wheeling financier and Northern Pacific Railroad owner, Henry Villard, didn't want to pay for the bridge, so in 1884 Union Pacific crossed the river into Oregon to meet the tracks of his Oregon Railway and Navigation Company. Soon a financial setback for Villard gave UP the line clear to Portland. Oregon remembers the financier today at the University of Oregon, where Villard Hall stands.

Huntington started out as a town divided between its family interests and the honky-tonk places, which made good money from the railroaders who rolled into town at all hours, and from cowboys who drove herds over the dusty trails to the railside cattle pens. A personal visit from Governor Oswald West finally helped to clean up the place. Many of the honky-tonks were shut down, and some members of the city council resigned. Huntington then settled down to railroading.

It was a town of only 700 people, but it had important railroad work to do. Historian Barbara Ruth Bailey describes the roundhouses at Huntington and La Grande:

> In these huge, circular buildings steam engine locomotives were maintained and repaired. This involved the region in a heavy industry of national scope, providing a town like Huntington with a regular payroll and a sense of purpose.

Huntington was also a division point, where orders were relayed, crews swapped, equipment checked, and engines changed. Those big engines were the key to Huntington.

Powerful locomotives were needed to blast their way into Oregon's Blue Mountains, while trains headed for Idaho required swift engines for the sagebrush plains. The pungent smoke of the big steamers was everywhere, and a Federal Writers' Project guidebook from Depression days describes Huntington's sun-parched houses, black train sheds, and smoke-stained trees. Still, all of that could be shrugged away as long as railroad paychecks staved off hard times.

Of course, Huntington knew firsthand that there was a Depression. Business activity affected both freight hauls and passenger traffic. Many travelers who, in earlier years, would have bought a ticket now shouldered a bedroll and tried to find a vacant boxcar, presumably headed where there was work.

The high councils of the Union Pacific organization were also wrestling with the Depression. Chairman W. A. Harriman had succeeded his father, the powerful railroad financier E. H. Harriman, in the executive suite. (W. A. Harriman went on to become governor of New York and ambassador to the USSR.) In 1933, he had said that a radically different train would be needed to hold passenger business. Huntington saw the result in 1935, when the first streamlined train glided into the yards. It was the *City of Portland*, a sleek aluminum tube in canary yellow and golden brown. No smoky engines hauled this train of the future. Instead, there were whirring diesels. On one of the first runs, the stop at Huntington was ten seconds. In some railroad towns, the train didn't stop at all.

Where was the casual talk at crew changes, the rough-and-ready life on the engines with their thundering blasts of coal smoke? Where was that steam whistle fading in the night that excited kids on back-road farms?

Travelers might have marveled at the fact that waiters could serve dinners when the train was clocking 80 miles per hour, and coffee and water wouldn't spill at 90 mph, but many steam railroaders of Huntington balked. Engineers signing on for the new equipment learned to operate the train without trouble, but asking firemen to transfer from coal to diesel engine work went against the grain, and they would change to a steam job when one showed up.

The streamliner, however, was a forecast of the future. In 1948, diesel began replacing all steam. It would only be a matter of time before trains rolled through Huntington without stopping.

# The Bonneville Dam Myth

HOLDING ONTO the myth of empire building during the Depression would have been contrary to reality. It had been 90 years since the first pioneers of the Oregon Trail ventured out from Missouri, and they had built well. But pioneer farms could be lost at a sheriff's sale for unpaid taxes, and many other enterprises gave way under financial pressure.

Amidst all this, another myth of sorts was introduced. It lingers in memory from a scratchy school-day film in black and white, of salmon leaping by the thousands up the churning rapids of the Columbia River. Then came a newer film, showing the fish swimming up stairstep ponds called ladders, which would take them safely past the great ramparts of Bonneville Dam, some 40 miles upstream from Portland.

Completed in 1938, Bonneville Dam was a large chunk of bright news in the Depression, the first dam on the mighty Columbia, the great "River of the West." The dam's huge turbines were ready to provide power so cheap that industry would be attracted to the Pacific Northwest from around the country.

Folk singer Woody Guthrie hailed the new era:


> Roll on, Columbia, roll on.
> Roll on, Columbia, roll on.
> Your power is turning our darkness to dawn,
> So roll on, Columbia, roll on.©


Freighting through the dam's locks would open up a new era in transportation. Other dams along the river would divert mighty quantities of water for irrigation, and their reservoirs would be useful in flood control. Bonneville Dam itself, a massive piece of construction, really was impressive, at a time when not much of anything was being built.

The salmon story was retold thousands of times to schoolchildren. The fish were hatched far inland, even in the mountain lakes of central Idaho. In time, they migrated to the Pacific Ocean, where they grew to impressive size. Finally, with incredible endurance, they returned inland, leaping the great rapids of the Columbia and its tributaries until, by some instinct, they reached the exact place where their lives had begun, to spawn the next generation.

This almost mythic kind of story, based on fact, was told for years. It was appealing because it promised constant renewing of the life forces in the Northwest.

It took decades for people to realize that the marvelous dams had delivered only part of their promised benefits — impressively so, but at the expense of the salmon, and more. It was the old story of people thinking they could reap the rewards of an enterprise without paying a price.

Over decades, the loss of salmon to the whirling turbines grew, until only a few were getting by. Only one ocean-going ship went through the Bonneville Dam locks and docked at The Dalles. On the other hand, cheap electricity did attract industry, especially large aluminum plants, and irrigation was expanded impressively, especially in central Washington. Barge traffic was developed on the river, and even Lewiston, Idaho, on the Snake River, became a seaport with direct water connections via the Columbia to the Pacific. For consumers, electrical power rates were low, and many liked boating or windsurfing on the reservoirs. Gone, however, were the pounding rapids where salmon once leaped upstream; the rocky ledges were sunk in quiet pools. On the entire stretch of dams along the Columbia River, from the Canadian border to Bonneville, only about 40 miles still are free-flowing.

# *Putting on a Show*

S OME OF the entertainment of the 1930s is bound to seem too pleasant and simple to today's reader. Amateur shows were popular and almost sure to feature a crowd of kids tap-dancing, the girls in short skirts which showed their skinny knees, and the boys in some kind of dress-up clothes that crimped their playground manners.

Tap-dancing suited the times. The lively music and the clattering taps set an upbeat tempo, which pushed aside the everyday drabness.

In between the troupes of entertainers there were solos,

often a young woman singing "My Sweet Little Alice Blue Gown," and some man with a deep voice imitating the notes of the double bass.

Jazz did not show up on these programs as a general rule. The only horn I recall hearing in our neighborhood was a bugle. As often was the case then, cost might have limited what was available. No doubt it explained the popularity of harmonicas. And jazz did not always get a welcome from professional musicians. I recall the story about the clarinet player at the Heilig Theater in Eugene during vaudeville years. When jazzy music was put on the program, he quit.

It was, of course, the younger generation that grabbed hold of jazz — the bright and brassy horns and the slamming drums. Parents threw up their hands in alarm over such a rowdy excuse for music.

Jazz seemed mixed up with the new swing music, which had a wider audience. Swing's bouncy kind of sound swept onto the popular scene in the middle of the Depression and added to youthful, upbeat entertainment. Parents naturally found it offensive when Benny Goodman turned Mendelssohn's "Spring Song," with its woodsy bird calls, into a jumping dance tune with a warbling clarinet.

As the 1940s began, even Tchaikovsky and Grieg piano concertos were abbreviated for dance bands into three-minute ripples of the keys, with saxophones tootling in the background. What of art, culture, refined sentiment, and the noble classics? The teens didn't care.

Mixed in with up-tempo swing music were dreamy songs like "Red Sails in the Sunset" and "Harbor Lights."

The big bands had a special effect on teen musicians. The kid who blasted out marches at the high school games could attempt the smooth trombone style of Tommy Dorsey, and come close enough to feel encouraged to practice more. In the swing era, instruments were played by young people who had taken music lessons, could read music, had played in school bands, and were encouraged by professional musicians. Popular music, including the kind on amateur hours, kept to its traditional roots.

Homegrown amateur hours no doubt were popular because they didn't cost much to stage — just a few prizes to the winners. They were boosted by a national radio program called the "Original Amateur Hour," with Major Edward Bowes as emcee. It featured voting by phone for the favorites and was immensely popular.

Radio's free entertainment provided a major pastime in the Depression. Although the more polished programs of network radio had been started a few years before the Depression, local stations had their own folksy humor shows and cowboy singers.

Before radio became popular in the 1920s, entertainment was live, except for phonograph records and movies; film sound was added in 1927, two years before the Depression, and Technicolor in 1932. It is difficult to realize that adults of the 1930s had grown up on a media mix consisting of newspapers, books, magazines, silent black and white films, and phonographs that were mechanical — wound up by a hand crank, with no electricity involved.

# Adventures in Kid Motoring

F INALLY, TOWARD the end of the Depression, came that unbelievably grand day when my buddy Tom put down $15, I think it was, and became the owner of a real automobile — four tires, a gearshift, and everything. He was probably the first kid in the neighborhood to ditch his bicycle. I still can picture that hulk of a khaki-colored sedan, bouncing along the ruts as Tom swung the wheel bravely. The car's special details, if memory serves, included wheels with wooden spokes and running boards for kids to jump onto. It was big and boxy, so the back seat riders could sit up straight and have plenty of room, an idea since declared outdated by the auto industry. Mechanically, Tom's car, in the familiar auto-lot expression, needed "a little work."

The newly motorized youth like Tom did not annoy my father, as I had thought they would.

"Let them go. They'll be good tank drivers in the next war," was the sort of remark he'd make as some kid roared down our street, spraying gravel.

Anyway, getting enough change to gas up Tom's car was the ongoing problem, but our empty pockets left plenty of time for working on the car, which meant puzzling over its worn parts. The fuel pump was a real problem when we tried to drive from here to there on a few splashes of gas in the tank. That is why we got into trouble with the law.

Short of gas one night, as usual, we had pulled into a station and counted our coin. It was embarrassing. Gas was 40 cents a gallon, and between us we could shake out only 10 cents. We asked for a dime's worth of gasoline.

A dime's worth! A quart of gasoline! The service station man had stormed in disgust. Drivers who were that broke shouldn't even be out on the road! But our request was legal, so he filled an empty milk bottle we had.

We didn't go far. The fuel pump wasn't pulling gas along from the tank, so we had to unscrew the fuel line and pour gas from the bottle directly into the pump, spilling some in the process. Then we started off.

A big mistake had been deciding to take our cruise in the evening, because among those parts of the car needing a little work were the electrical items. We could have held a couple of flashlights out the window and done a better job than the headlights. We were away from traffic, probably hoping we wouldn't attract attention, when the law noticed our shadowy progress and pulled us over.

As soon as the policeman reached Tom's window, the powerful smell of raw gas, a siphon hose, and a can in the back seat put the officer onto something more serious. It looked like a "midnight requisitioning" of someone else's gas had been going on. Tom told the skeptical officer the truth, and later told it to a judge, who gave him a fair hearing, though I think he had to pay a small fine, perhaps for the headlights. Of course, any amount would have seemed drastic then, especially to youthful motorists who bought gas by the quart.

# *Portland on the Upbeat*

OWNTOWN PORTLAND had an upbeat side in the late 1930s, though given the times, that may sound impossible. Of course, everything is either exciting or boring when you're young and carefree. Memory overlooks everyday happenings, like getting soaked in the pouring rain.

But downtown Portland was a lively and eventful place (though "eventful," at that age, might have meant finding good coconut cream pie for 15 cents a slice). What was different was that there were no malls; almost everything was downtown, where a hundred and one stores and shops were run by their owners and, maybe, some hired help. Each place had a personality, whether casual or hustling. No two were alike. Customers had to explore, ask questions, get involved, give new things a try. Every hamburger, every chocolate sundae was different and distinct, in never-ending variety, and the same applied to many other items.

Downtown Portland was a noisy place. Newspaper headlines were shouted from the corners as the *Oregonian*, *Oregon Journal*, and *News-Telegram* rolled each new edition off the presses. Streetcar bells clanged as pedestrians scurried across the cobblestones, urged on by rolling blasts from a traffic cop's whistle. Noise excites youth; downtown Portland had plenty of it.

Admission to the movies was a dime, and cowboys always rode around the same rock and tied their horses at the same saloon. Somehow on these movie ranges, the horses never stirred up much dust, unless Gabby Hayes was supposed to squint into the distance and say, "Who's that headed thisaway pow'ful fast?" Of course everybody knew it was the sheriff, because the bad guys always went "thataway." Still, cowboying seemed like a good occupation, according to the motion pictures. Nobody did any work; the cowhands just sat around listening to the Sons of the Pioneers.

Even as the Depression seemed to be ending (and there was nothing special marking that long-awaited time), high schoolers didn't have much to spend, though people at the little shops were always glad to plunk a few more dimes in the cash drawer. I recall that a new place on Broadway became the popular Coca-Cola stop after school, but soon went out of business. Talk was that the way teenagers could stretch out the sipping of a single Coke kept the crowd thick but the profits thin.

There was some free entertainment downtown. At music

counters, you could hand a piece of sheet music to a pianist and the melody would ripple through the store. Down by the Willamette River, you could watch the drawbridges open in whistled sequence as some high-masted craft churned by. And sometimes downtown a new car would drive past, looking just like the pictures in the magazines.

In a department store window there might be a colorful make-believe fall scene from some campus, the rah-rah boys waving their pennants for the team and the cheerleader girls swinging their short skirts, while the spectators showed the latest fall fashions. It was a somewhat dreamy scene, because most high schoolers didn't go to college then. The closest many could get to a college game was to hear it on the radio.

The upbeat experience of downtown Portland in the late 1930s might begin with swinging down from a big red-and-cream interurban trolley and into the crowds, perhaps on a rainy afternoon when neon made the steamy windows a foggy red and blue. At the Orpheum Theater, strings of bright lights circled around the title of the latest movie, "The Adventures of Robin Hood," with Olivia De Havilland making Maid Marian much more interesting than the library books, in late-night whisperings with the stealthy Robin, otherwise known as Errol Flynn.

Stores on Broadway were crammed with the latest, like those cream-colored cords the college boys wore until the pants were so dirty it was said they could be stood in a corner — that was the fad. And stores had anything you could name: rare coins, colorful stamps, candid cameras, glittering rings, mountains of chocolates, shiny shoes, and clothes for rich people. The man in the window display wearing a woolly suit with a vest, and the woman in something silky in waves of exotic colors were like a preview of some grand and nearby future.

# *Building the Empire Again*

WORLD WAR II changed everything. The thunder was heard from overseas late in the 1930s, and even if American public opinion said "Stay out," some increase in U.S. armaments took place in 1939. Historians hold differing viewpoints on what caused the Depression, but they generally agree that this rearmament ended the hard times.

Industrialist Henry Kaiser built shipyards in Portland and across the Columbia River in Vancouver and started hiring. (He was also a major player in the construction of Boulder/

Hoover, Bonneville, Shasta, and Grand Coulee Dams, plus steel and aluminum mills.) Soon he was recruiting on the East Coast, sending trainloads of workers west to good jobs at good pay. The story goes that prospective employees were told they only had to know which was the business end of a wrench, and if they didn't know, it would be labeled for them.

The solid paychecks that had been dreamed of for years were a reality, and the good times began to roll, though given bittersweet twists by partings as soldiers went to war. Still, there were brave hopes for the future, for a time when prosperity would let Oregon's empire building begin again.

Now, in schools of the 1990s, the Depression is being studied — often, unfortunately, by means of literature. Much of literature's absorbing quality is gained by putting characters in unreal but dramatic situations. In many ways the Depression provided the opposite, because it had so many limitations on doing, building, spending, and trying out new ideas. The result was caution. There was no room for risk-taking. When prosperity returned, optimism opened the door to opportunities. Depression-era days were not the stuff of high drama, but gritty determination.

Recently, I have heard some people who lived through the Depression say it might be a good idea if the country had another one — the implied reason being to let Americans get back to the basics and away from remote-controlled gizmos to open garage doors, exotic vacations on borrowed money, grapes in winter from another continent, and automobiles with powered side mirrors.

But I think that people who wish for a Depression to straighten out the country really don't mean what they say. If they thought of the dangers involved, I presume they would change their minds.

We must remember that no way out of the Depression was

found. Rearmament was not a planned solution, but a response to world-power politics.

No, a Depression is too severe a remedy for real or supposed national problems. However, ours of the 1930s is worth studying, and its lessons need more attention from world policymakers.

The start of the 1930s Depression meant the end of empire building by the independent kind of people who had braved the Oregon Trail. When the federal government took the responsibility for keeping people employed, paying the jobless, funding retirement, and building dams to attract industry, a whole new, less independent lifestyle developed. It had been a long time coming, but it probably was inevitable after the experiences that people of the 1930s somehow endured.

# Goodbye to the Neighborhood

HAVING GOT through the Depression, the independent neighborhood of Errol Heights seemed able to withstand anything. Yet one day I read that it was gone. Portland had annexed this rural acreage on its boundary, and now called by what I deemed the impossibly grand name of Brentwood-Darlington. There were objections at the time from people in Portland; some didn't want that neighborhood added to the city's reputation. But county officials had run out of funds to provide the usual services, so Portland got Errol Heights. Annexation took place in stages between 1964 and 1986.

I walked through the neighborhood in the mid-1960s, as annexation was beginning, and found that little had changed. The gravel street in front of our house had been paved, although my parents were annoyed about the cost. My mother was still cooking on a woodstove. Most places had telephones. Overall, people seemed cautious, despite the general prosperity. It was as though they still saw the ragged edge of the Depression cloud far off, and for them it never would go away.

I have made several visits since then, still not observing much change. The scenes do bring back memories, of the brushy lots where we gathered hazelnuts and then sat around cracking them and chattering like squirrels; there were wild blackberries, too, with a taste like sweet wine.

The towering firs are still there, though the paving at last has replaced the mud puddles.

The houses still seem in reasonably good shape, but after many years of wear, they had rented cheaply and had attracted people who were problems for the law. However, since annexation, more than 42 neighborhood watches have been established, a park restored, traffic control improved, and home burglaries brought down by 46 percent, according to a city official.

When I lived in Errol Heights as a boy, burglaries were unheard of; there wouldn't have been much to steal. I can recall money being so scarce that the insurance agent called regularly for the payment of a dime on a policy, which was carefully receipted. A dime also bought a quart of milk then. Where the money came from to celebrate the holidays puzzles me, but they were observed happily. And I remember a sight to startle any fire marshal: real candles burning on a fir Christmas tree in the home of neighbors from Germany.

We didn't think of ourselves as poor in Errol Heights, and I can't actually recall the word being used. We brought coins to school so that the Community Chest could help the less fortunate.

The subsequent industrial boom of World War II gave most of the Portland-area men a chance to pull down a good paycheck, and, as more men were drafted, women took up all kinds of work. My mother put her training as a registered nurse to use.

But after 1937, when I had gone to a high school across town, I was away most of the day and didn't hear much about what was happening in the neighborhood.

Still, my opinions and attitudes were certainly shaped by having grown up there. I don't admire tacky clothes as a fad — in the '30s, we kept up appearances. I don't understand going bankrupt from overspending. It's difficult to accept the fact that people join diet clubs because they have too much to eat, and then give control over their weight to someone else. I am baffled by the emphasis that people put on being "comfortable" with situations, as though that was an achievement.

The people of Errol Heights in the '30s would undoubtedly have liked some recent ideas: garage sales, heating systems to warm a house better than a woodstove could, wash-and-wear fabrics, and penicillin. But I wonder about how our neighbors in the Depression years would have reacted to the impressive name of Brentwood-Darlington. It might have been too much for those common sense 1930s people of Errol Heights.

Updated lifestyles in new settings have left many neighborhoods on the old streetcar lines behind. It takes some imagining to picture Errol Heights as the "natural park" which that newspaper writer described 80 years ago. True, the same tall firs spear the sky and the view from our old street, which runs along the top of a hill, recalls walks past tawny fields sloping down to a creek which wound almost wild through alder, willow, wild cherry, and maple.

And somewhere there still must be flowers in the spring, where hazelnut trees bend in brushy arches, shading pale lavender spring beauties, white trilliums, purple flags of iris, and Oregon Grape, in a remembered setting for hard times and for good times.

# *Sources*

AILEY, BARBARA Ruth. *Main Street North-eastern Oregon* (Portland: Oregon Historical Society Press, 1982), 34.

Bureau of the Census. *Historical Statistics of the United States: Colonial Times to 1970* (Washington, D.C.: U.S. Government Printing Office, 1975), Part 1, 33. (The basis of data collection was changed for 1950, so comparisons are uncertain when they involve years before then and recent times.)

Federal Writers' Project. *The Oregon Trail* (New York:

Hastings House, 1939), 124.

Guthrie, Woody. "Roll On, Columbia." Words by Woody Guthrie, music based on "Goodnight, Irene," by Huddie Ledbetter and John A. Lomax. Copyright 1936 (renewed), 1957 (renewed), and 1963 (renewed), Ludlow Music, Inc., New York, NY. Used with permission.

Hofstadter, Richard. *The American Political Tradition* (New York: Vintage, 1948), 331-332.

Lindley, William R. "Huntington, Oregon, Railroad History," *Journal of the West*, Oct. 1991, 36-44.

Lindley, William R. "Lumber King Countered Wobblies with Portland Trade School," *Journal of the West*, Oct. 1993, 69-75.

Lindley, William R. "On Portland's Boundary Line: Errol Heights in the Trying Thirties," *Journal of the West*, Jan. 1990, 62-66.

MacColl, E. Kimbark. *The Growth of a City* (Portland, OR: Georgian Press, 1979), 268.

Nielsen, George R. *The Danish Americans* (Boston: Twayne, 1981), 168.

O'Donnell, Terence. *That Balance So Rare: The Story of Oregon* (Portland: Oregon Historical Society Press, 1988), 101.

*Oregonian* (Portland), Nov. 16, 1913, section 4, 12.

# A Note on Photographs

THE PHOTOGRAPHS in this book depict scenes typical of the Depression years, though not all were taken during the 1930s. The names of the people shown are generally unavailable.

Good scenes from those years are difficult to find; many photos presumably are in family albums, not public collections. I was not able to find a good photograph of the neighborhood where I grew up. Today, of course, such photos would have historical value, but 60 years ago no one would have thought to take a picture of some scattered houses on a rough street.

Fortunately, the Oregon Historical Society's photo collection has considerable range; perhaps readers will want to donate good prints of general interest to that organization.

Anyway, for these reasons, the photographs in this book are intended only to give an impression of the times.

# Illustrations

By the 1930s, Portland had a trim skyline, but the future was on hold. (OrHi 46360)

Some were doing all right, as new homes in Eastmoreland showed. (CN 020244)

Some built in Sullivan's Gulch, on the tracks east of the Steel Bridge. (COP 00152)

Men lined up outside of Grandma's Kitchen at Front and Columbia Streets, Portland, about 1930. (CN 010148)

There was always time to talk things over downtown at S.W. 2nd Avenue and Madison. (OrHi 38902)

Produce stands on Yamhill Street were always noisy with friendly banter. (CN 024195)

For light shopping there was the corner store — this one at 74th and Glisan. (CN 020938)

Develoyments of the great Columbia River caught on in the 1930s. (CN 016283)

The roundhouse at Huntington, where Union Pacific changed old habits. (OrHi 15901)

A big mallet engine swings through Eugene on a Southern Pacific run. (OrHi 44774)

Explorers flank the entrance to the Oregon capitol at Salem. The legend says, "Westward the Star of Empire Takes Its Way." (OrHi 42956)

Covered wagon emigrants and a pioneer on the rotunda complete the theme: "Valiant Men Have Thrust Our Frontiers to the Setting Sun." (OrHi 57785)

The settled Willamette Valley showed small fields and groves of trees. (OrHi 80289)

Mount Hood, a sentinel for pioneers, still provides a dramatic backdrop. (OrHi 15838)

A team in the field near Sheridan recalls early farming, and Depression economies. (OrHi 35711)

The Rose Festival parade on June 14, 1931, drew crowds to downtown Portland. (OrHi 67093)

Portland was at its best, flags flying, for the American Legion Convention, September 11, 1932. (CN 001850)

Life was simple in the 1930s. Service was personal, clothes were practical.
(CN 009481)

For many thousands, hope turned to bleakness on the sidewalks of Portland. (OrHi 60061)

This tells the whole story! (OrHi 12881)

# Index